# FLYING REPTILES

## BY
## S.L. HAMILTON

A&D Xtreme
An imprint of Abdo Publishing | www.abdopublishing.com

abdopublishing.com

Published by Abdo Publishing, a division of ABDO, PO Box 398166, Minneapolis, Minnesota 55439. Copyright ©2018 by Abdo Consulting Group, Inc. International copyrights reserved in all countries. No part of this book may be reproduced in any form without written permission from the publisher. A&D Xtreme™ is a trademark and logo of Abdo Publishing.

Printed in the United States of America, North Mankato, MN.
092017
012018

Editor: John Hamilton
Graphic Design: Sue Hamilton
Cover Design: Candice Keimig and Pakou Vang
Cover Photo: iStock
Interior Photos & Illustrations: Alamy-pgs 6, 16-17, 20-21, 27 & 28-29; American Museum of Natural History-pgs 13 (inset) & 26 (bottom); AP-pgs 18-19; Gabriel Lio-pg 24; Getty-pgs 22-23; Glow Images-pgs 30-31; iStock-pgs 7, 24 (background) & 31 (inset); Mark Witton and Darren Naish-pg 19 (inset); Maurilio Oliveira/Museu Nacional-UFRJ/PA-pg 25; Reuters-pg 32; Science Source-pgs 8-9, 10-11, 14-15 & 15 (left inset); Shutterstock-pgs 1, 2-3, 4-5, 10 (inset), 12, 15 (right inset); Travis Shinabarger-pgs 12-13; Wikimedia-pgs 13 (inset) & 30 (inset); Xiaolin Wang-pg 26 (top)

Publisher's Cataloging-in-Publication Data

Names: Hamilton, S.L., author.
Title: Flying reptiles / by S.L. Hamilton.
Description: Minneapolis, Minnesota : Abdo Publishing, 2018. | Series: Xtreme Dinosaurs | Includes online resources and index.
Identifiers: LCCN 2017946692 | ISBN 9781532112942 (lib.bdg.) | ISBN 9781532150807 (ebook)
Subjects: LCSH: Pterosauria--Juvenile literature. | Prehistoric animals--Juvenile literature. | Dinosaurs--Juvenile literature. | Paleontology--Juvenile literature.
Classification: DDC 567.918--dc23
LC record available at https://lccn.loc.gov/2017946692

# CONTENTS

Flying Reptiles ......................................................... 4

Types ..................................................................... 6

Wings ..................................................................... 8

Tails ...................................................................... 10

Teeth...................................................................... 12

Head Crests ............................................................ 16

Largest Pterosaurs .................................................. 18

Smallest Pterosaurs ................................................ 22

Newly Discovered Pterosaurs .................................... 24

Nesting .................................................................. 26

Extinction............................................................... 28

Glossary.................................................................. 30

Online Resources ..................................................... 31

# FLYING REPTILES

Pterosaurs were not dinosaurs, but lived at the same time. These "winged lizards" soared in the skies during the Mesozoic era. They lived from about 215 million to 65 million years ago.

*Anhanguera*
*(Old Devil)*

**XTREME FACT – Pterosaurs were the first creatures, after insects, that could lift themselves from the Earth and fly using their own power.**

Pterosaurs were reptiles whose arms and bodies were covered in stretched skin. They were not the ancestors of birds, but they did have hollow, air-filled bones that allowed them to fly. They hunted fish, small dinosaurs, eggs, and insects from prehistoric Earth's skies.

# TYPES

The first pterosaurs were smaller-sized flying reptiles with long tails. They were known as rhamphorhynchoids, or "beak snouts."

*XTREME FACT – Pterosaurs are often called "pterodactyls." However, pterodactyls are just one type of pterosaur.*

During the 150 million years that pterosaurs soared in the skies, these flying reptiles evolved into larger creatures with smaller tails and bigger brains. This group is known as pterodactyloids, or "winged fingers."

# WINGS

Pterosaur wings were made up of thin membranes of skin, muscle, and stiffening fibers. The end of each wing had three movable fingers. A fourth very long finger held the side of the wing.

Instead of constantly flapping their wings, pterosaurs likely glided with their wings outstretched. By riding thermals, going from one column of rising warm air to another, they could stay aloft without needing to move their wings, much like today's large birds, such as vultures.

XTREME FACT – A pterosaur's very long fourth finger is known as the megafinger.

# TAILS

Early pterosaurs
had long tails. It
is believed the tails
helped with directional
movement, much like
a rudder on a plane. The
ends of the tails were either
forked, or equipped with a
diamond- or triangle-shaped tip.
These are known as "tail vanes."
The tails may also have been a way
to attract mates.

**XTREME FACT** – Sordes pilosus *had the longest tail-to-body size of any pterosaur. Its tail was twice as long as its body.*

As millions of years passed, pterosaur tails became smaller and smaller. Scientists are still trying to understand why pterosaurs had tails and why they nearly disappeared.

# TEETH

Pterosaur teeth varied widely depending on the species. *Dimorphodon*, an early pterosaur that likely ate insects, had a large head with a puffin-like beak. Its teeth were spiky in front and small in back.

*Dimorphodon
(Two-Form
Tooth)*

*The African
pterosaur had spiky
interlocking teeth that allowed
it to trap fish inside its mouth.*

*Pterodaustro* had a mouth filled with sieve-like teeth. It probably flew over water and skimmed off the small

*Pterodaustro*
(Wing From
The South)

creatures and vegetation near the surface. *Dsungaripterus weii* had a curved, pointy jaw that could pry shellfish off rocks, and peg-like teeth that could crush the shells.

*Dsungaripterus weii*
(Wing honoring C.M. Wei)

Unlike other pterosaurs, *Pteranodons* had long, toothless beaks. Scientists guess that this pterosaur may have fished by skimming the water's surface with an open beak. Or it may have fished from the surface of the water, diving down to capture its meal. It may also have been a scavenger, using its beak to reach in and snap off pieces of dead dinosaurs.

*Pteranodon*
(Wing Without Tooth)

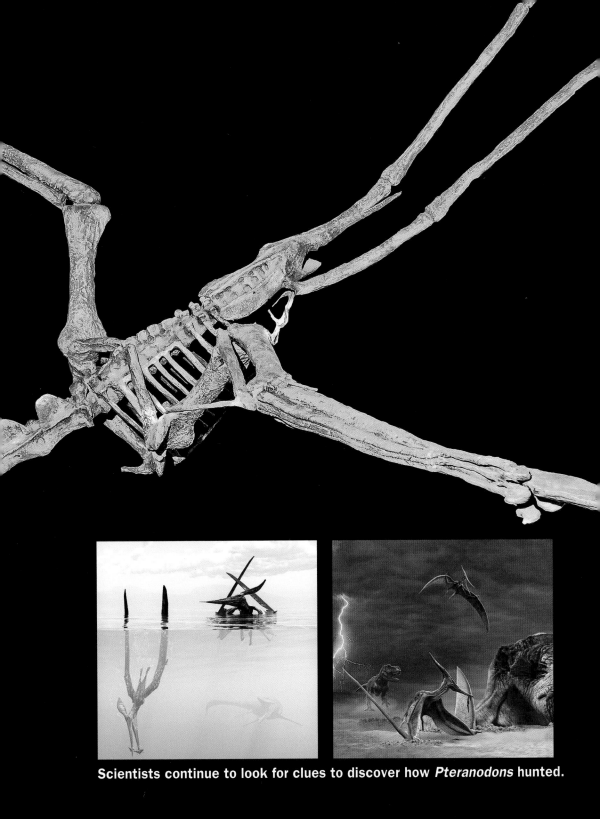

Scientists continue to look for clues to discover how *Pteranodons* hunted.

# HEAD CRESTS

Pterosaurs often had large crests on their heads. It is likely that the lightweight hollow bone helped balance the pterosaur's long jaw and keep its head upright.

*Tupandactylus imperator*
**(Tupan Finger Emperor)**

Scientists also guess that the crests acted as rudders, aiding in flight. Or the crests may have helped warm or cool the pterosaur's temperature. The variety of pterosaur crests suggests that it also may have been used to help the species attract mates.

*XTREME FACT – Tupandactylus imperator had one of the largest sail-like crests of any pterosaur. The huge crest may have been used to signal other pterosaurs or to frighten enemies, much like today's large-billed toucan birds.*

# LARGEST
# PTEROSAURS

*Quetzalcoatlus northropi* was one of
the largest flying reptiles known. It
stood 20 feet (6 m) tall, as tall as an
adult giraffe. Its wingspan was 36 to
40 feet (11 to 12 m) across. Once
in the air, the great wings may have
propelled the pterosaur to speeds of
more than 67 miles per hour (108 kph).

The huge
**Quetzalcoatlus
northropi** *stood
as tall as a
giraffe.*

*Hatzegopteryx*
(Hateg Basin Wing)

**Hatzegopteryx** had a wingspan of 33 to 36 feet (10 to 11 m). Its skull was 10 feet (3 m) long. It was so big and heavy that it may have needed a running start to take off from land. It hunted small dinosaurs.

XTREME FACT – Because pterosaurs had light, hollow bones, it is rare for their fragile bodies to have survived long enough to become fossilized.

# SMALLEST PTEROSAURS

*Nemicolopterus crypticus* is one of the smallest flying reptiles known. Fossil remains found in China show the toothless pterosaur was about the size of a sparrow. Its wingspan reached only 10 inches (25 cm) across.

*Nemicolopterus crypticus*
(Hidden Flying Forest Dweller)

*Nemicolopterus* lived about 120 million years ago. Its curved foot bones lead scientists to believe that it lived in trees. It may have been an inland forest-dweller, instead of a shoreline pterosaur. It likely hunted and ate insects.

*XTREME FACT – Some pterosaurs had furry, hair-like coverings, known as pycnofibers, on their bodies and wings.*

# Newly Discovered Pterosaurs

In 2016, paleontologists discovered a new long-tailed pterosaur in Argentina, South America. Parts of *Allkaruen koi's* head are so well preserved that scientists can study the anatomy of its brain.

*Allkaruen koi*
(Ancient Brain
From The Lake)

A group of 47 *Caiuajara dobruskii* fossils were unearthed in Brazil, South America, in 2011. Males were large, with 16-foot (5-m) wingspans. Females were half the size of males. Because they were found all together in one place, it is believed they lived as a family.

*Caiuajara dobruskii* (Caiuá Group geologic formation and honors the finder, Alexandre Dobruski)

# Nesting

A pterosaur egg found in China.

Pterosaurs likely created nesting areas near water. The mothers buried their leathery, soft-shelled eggs in moist sand, much like turtles do today. Scientists believe the babies, or "flaplings," could fly shortly after hatching. Their wings were big enough to allow flight from the start of their lives.

A baby pterosaur fossil still in its egg. Newly hatched babies are called "flaplings."

*Tupuxuara leonardii*
(Long-Crested and honoring
Giuseppe Leonardi)

*A pterosaur provides
food for its baby.*

**XTREME FACT** – No one knew for sure if pterosaurs
laid eggs or had live births until a fossil of a pterosaur
mother with an egg in her was found in China in 2004.

# EXTINCTION

Over the course of 150 million years, species of flying reptiles grew and changed. However, about 66 million years ago, a world-changing event occurred. It may have been asteroids striking the Earth. Perhaps volcanoes began erupting.

Climate may have changed. Diseases may have struck. It may have been a number of things. Scientists continue to look for clues to explain the mass extinction of flying reptiles, dinosaurs, and other prehistoric animals.

*XTREME FACT – Pterosaurs flew in Earth's skies for 50 million years before the coming of the first bird, Archaeopteryx.*

# GLOSSARY

**EVOLVE**
To change over time. Living things may change in shape, size, or other ways to make life better for future generations.

**EXTINCT**
When every member of a specific living thing has died. Pterosaurs are extinct.

**FOSSILS**
The preserved remains or imprints of prehistoric animals or plants in stone.

**MEMBRANE**
A thin, soft, sheet of skin and other materials that make up the wings of a pterosaur.

**MESOZOIC ERA**
A time in Earth's history from about 245 million years ago to 65 million years ago. Dinosaurs roamed the Earth at this time. This overall era includes the Triassic, Jurassic, and Cretaceous periods.

**QUETZALCOATL**
The Aztec creator god pictured as a feathered serpent. According to myth, he helped create the world, brought learning, and gave corn to humanity.

### Rudder

A movable, flat piece of a plane or boat that helps steer the craft. A pterosaur's tail vane and crest were thought to act as rudders for the flying reptile.

### Snout

The nose and mouth areas of an animal.

### Thermals

Rising columns of warm air. Pterosaurs, like some of today's birds, likely rode thermals, which allowed them to stay aloft without flapping their wings.

## ONLINE RESOURCES

**Booklinks**
NONFICTION NETWORK
FREE! ONLINE NONFICTION RESOURCES

To learn more about Xtreme Dinosaurs, visit abdobooklinks.com. These links are routinely monitored and updated to provide the most current information available.

# INDEX

*Tropeognathus cf. T. mesembrinus*
*(Keel Jaw of the South)*

## A
African pterosaur  12
*Allkaruen koi*  24
*Anhanguera*  4
*Archaeopteryx*  29
Argentina, South
   America  24

## B
Brazil, South America
   25

## C
Caiuá Group (geologic
   formation)  25
*Caiuajara dobruskii*  25
China  22, 26, 27
crest  16, 17

## D
*Dimorphodon*  12
Dobruski, Alexandre  25
*Dsungaripterus weii*  13

## E
Earth  4, 5, 28, 29

## F
flaplings  26

## G
giraffe  18, 19

## H
*Hatzegopteryx*  20

## L
Leonardi, Giuseppe  27

## M
megafinger  9
Mesozoic era  4

## N
*Nemicolopterus
   crypticus*  22, 23
Northrop, John  18, 19

## P
*Pteranodon*  14, 15
pterodactyl  6
pterodactyloids  7
*Pterodaustro*  13
puffin (bird)  12
pycnofibers  23

## Q
Quetzalcoatl (Aztec god)
   18, 19
*Quetzalcoatlus northropi*
   18, 19

## R
rhamphorhynchoids  6
rudder  10, 17

## S
*Sordes pilosus*  10
South America  24, 25
sparrow  22

## T
tail vanes  10
thermals  9
toucan  17
*Tropeognathus cf. T.
   mesembrinus*  32
*Tupandactylus imperator*
   16, 17
*Tupuxuara leonardii*  27
turtle  26

## V
vulture  9